P9-DII-782

**First edition for the United States
and Canada published in 1999 by
Barron's Educational Series, Inc.**

Copyright © 1998 Ringpress Books

PHOTOGRAPHS: Amanda Bulbeck
All rights reserved.

No part of this book may be reproduced in any form, by
photostat, microfilm, xerography, or any other means,
or incorporated into any information retrieval system,
electronic or mechanical, without the written permission
of the copyright owner.

All inquiries should be addressed to:
Barron's Educational Series, Inc.
250 Wireless Boulevard
Hauppauge,New York 11788
http://www.barronseduc.com

International Standard Book No. 0-7641-1003-9
Library of Congress Catalog Card No. 98-73925
Printed in Hong Kong. 9 8 7 6 5 4 3 2 1

BARRON'S

All About Your

COCKATIEL

Bradley Viner

Contents

Introduction

The cockatiel is a small member of the parrot family that is midway in size between a budgerigar and larger parrots such as the African Gray. If you are interested in keeping a cockatiel as a pet, or already have some experience, but would like to learn more about them, then this book is for you. We will concentrate on keeping one or two birds indoors, rather than the more serious hobby of maintaining an aviary.

Understanding Cockatiels

Cockatiels are cheerful and intelligent companions and their gentle nature makes them ideal pets for someone who has the time to devote to caring for them. They are much quieter and less aggressive than many other members of the parrot family. They are inexpensive to purchase and maintain, and are not generally prone to illness. They are suitable for older children to look after, but the dust that they produce means that they should not be looked after by someone suffering from asthma, and certainly not kept in their bedroom.

Cockatiels are intelligent and their gentle nature makes them ideal pets.

The cockatiel is now the third most popular pet bird, after budgerigars and canaries. However, if it is a talking bird that you are after, then you are unlikely to be satisfied with a cockatiel. Although they can be trained to talk, they are generally overshadowed by larger parrots such as the African Gray, or even by the humble budgerigar. Pet birds were once confined to their cages, often alone, for their entire lives. Today, people are more enlightened, and most owners realize that pet birds should either be allowed plenty of opportunity to fly outside the confines of their cage, or be kept in a group in an aviary that provides enough space for them to fly around freely. Since the cockatiel grows to about 12 inches (30 cm) in length, it needs a sizeable aviary if it is not allowed to fly around indoors.

DID YOU KNOW?

The Latin name for the cockatiel is *Nymphicus hollandicus.*

How Many?

As cockatiels are naturally sociable in the wild, it seems that a pair of birds is ideal for a pet owner and, provided they grow up together, two birds of either sex will be good companions. A cock and a hen are also fine, and you may have the added delight of happy families of cockatiels, but you have to be prepared to find good homes for the regular clutches of offspring.

Cockatiels can be mixed with other species of birds in an aviary, and are usually fine even with considerably smaller birds such as canaries or other members of the finch family. You should keep a single bird only if you are certain you will be able to give it all the human companionship that it needs to replace that of other members of its own species. Boredom is a very serious problem among pet birds and can lead to distressing signs such as self-mutilation.

Cockatiels are naturally sociable and enjoy each other's company.

Varieties of Cockatiel

Gray

The gray, or normal variety of cockatiel is very similar to the wild bird, with a lighter body color on the underside. The forehead, cheeks, and throat are lemon-yellow bordered with white, and the ear coverts are orange.

The adult male has much brighter facial colors than the female, and a much more prominent yellow and gray crest, which can stand up on its end at will. The female is often more slimly built, and the underside of the tail feathers are crossed with dull yellow bands. Immature birds are all similar to the females, so it can be difficult to distinguish the sexes until the male matures.

The gray cockatiel has a lighter body color on the underside.

Pied

The first variety to develop in captivity was the pied, which has patches of white within the normal plumage.

Lutino

The most common domestic variety is the lutino. It lacks any black

The pied cockatiel.

DID YOU KNOW?

Outside the breeding season when they pair off, cockatiels live in communal flocks, eating mainly seeds of grasses and other plants.

pigment in its feathers, so its body plumage is completely white instead of gray. Unlike the gray, the female is more attractive than the male, with a richer, deeper yellow head coloration.

Albino
The albino cockatiel has no coat pigment at all and so is pure white all over.

The Lutino has white body plumage.

Pearl
Pearl cockatiels were first bred in Germany in 1967 and have a very appealing scalloped pattern.

Cinnamon and Silver
These color variations are now also becoming available.

The choice of color is very much a matter of personal preference, as all varieties are identical in terms of their suitability as pets.

The normal and lutino variants are the most common, and are likely to be the least costly to purchase.

DID YOU KNOW?

The parrot family varies in size from pygmy parrots, which at 4 inches (10 cm) body length are smaller than sparrows, to the giant hyacinthine macaw, which can reach an overall length of 39 inches (100 cm).

Buying a Cockatiel

A male cockatiel (left) and a female.

Most pet stores supply cockatiels, or you could go to a breeder, who may be happy to sell you birds that are unsuitable for showing and breeding but will make perfect pets. If you go to a pet store, make sure it is one that has a good reputation, is well kept, and where all the stock looks healthy and well maintained, and are not overcrowded.

Some shops specialize in the sale of pet birds, and the staff is likely to have a greater knowledge about bird-keeping than a more general store.

Male or Female?

It is not possible to tell the sex of young cockatiels, so you will have to buy adults if you want to be certain of getting a breeding pair. Otherwise, get the youngest cockatiel possible, provided it is old enough to leave the nest. Young birds less than about three months of age generally have pinkish-colored beaks. After six months of age, the stripes on the chest will become less prominent and the plumage differences between the sexes will become obvious.

DID YOU KNOW?

The correct name for the keeping or rearing of birds is aviculture, after the Latin word *avis* for bird.

Signs of a Healthy Cockatiel

Eyes: bright and clear.

Feathers: sleek and well preened.

Body condition: plump.

Breathing: rapid, but quiet.

Vent: a single opening common to the digestive, urinary, and reproductive tracts, which should be clean.

Behavior: chirpy and bold.

DID YOU KNOW?

Members of the parrot family (which includes cockatiels) have been kept for thousands of years as pets. The Roman author Pliny gave detailed instructions on how to teach a parrot to talk in the first century A.D. The demand for parrots in Rome even reached the point where they were sold for more than the cost of a human slave, and were kept in cages made of ivory and silver.

Setting Up a Home

DID YOU KNOW?

Birds are very susceptible to poisoning by fumes, which is why miners used to take canaries down into the mines. They should be removed from the room if there is a lot of cigarette smoke or an open fire. Even the fumes from an overheated non-stick saucepan can be highly toxic to a cockatiel.

Keeping a cockatiel in a cage for most of its life is not fulfilling either for the bird or for you as its owner. Unless you have a large aviary in which several birds can be allowed to fly freely, you should only keep "caged" birds if you are able to allow them regular access to a safe area where they can fly around.

Do not purchase a cage designed for budgerigars or canaries for a cockatiel. Cockatiels are about twice the size and need much more space. The larger the cage, the better, particularly if you are keeping more than one bird or if it is to spend a considerable proportion of the day confined. The minimum is an 18-inch (46 cm) square base that is 24 inches (61 cm) high. Cockatiels do seem to like climbing upward and downward, so a tall cage rather than a wide one is best, and one with a rectangular base is preferable to a round one. Buy a sturdy cage that is designed with a pull-out tray base that holds the loose bird sand or sheets of sandpaper, so that it is easy to clean. Make sure there is no plastic within reach of the bird that can be pecked and splintered.

Placing the Cage

Do not position the cage in direct sunlight, or in a draft. The cage should be covered at night to keep in the warmth, and to prevent the birds from being startled if someone

Do not position the cage in direct sunlight.

switches on the lights. Some house plants are poisonous to birds, and should be removed or covered when the birds are allowed out unattended.

On its first excursions there is a danger that the bird may fly into a window and injure itself, so the curtains should be closed and any open fires guarded. The doors to the room can be protected with a bead or net curtain to prevent the bird from flying out if it is accidentally left open. In many households, birds can be left to fly free all day, being shut into their cage only at night.

DID YOU KNOW?

The cockatiel has three eyelids – an upper, a lower, and a third eyelid that it can pull across the eye from the side to protect it.

Setting Up a Home

Fixtures and Fittings

Cages will generally come supplied with perches, a wooden swing, and food and water bowls.

PERCHES:
The standard bar that is usually supplied as a perch is too narrow for many cockatiels. Lengths of fruit tree branches, with varying thickness, make much better perches, as the birds can choose what suits them best.

FLOOR COVERING:
The floor of the cage can be covered with sand, but most owners find it more convenient to use the disposable sandpaper .

TOYS:
Cockatiels do enjoy toys – especially trying to eat them! It is better to supply a new toy each day in rotation rather than cluttering the cage with a wide variety of toys. Something as simple as a Ping-Pong ball can

Cockatiels appreciate perches of varying thickness.

provide hours of fun. Bells and mirrors are also extremely popular. Plastic can sometimes splinter when pecked, so wooden toys may be best.

Some owners even make mobile gyms for their cockatiels that can be moved from one room to another. These consist of a sturdy wooden base with a selection of perches, swings, and ladders and some swinging toys for the cockatiels to peck at.

These can provide hours of fun for the birds, as well as entertainment for their owners.

DID YOU KNOW?

Cockatiels are warm-blooded, with a normal body temperature of about 106°F (41°C), considerably higher than that of domestic pets such as cats and dogs.

Cockatiels are bright and inquisitive, and they enjoy playing with toys.

Seeds

Cockatiels eat mainly seeds in the wild, naturally consuming a wide variety of seed types as different plants come into season. However, an all-seed diet tends to be high in fat and provides an unbalanced source of nutrients that can lead to ill health.

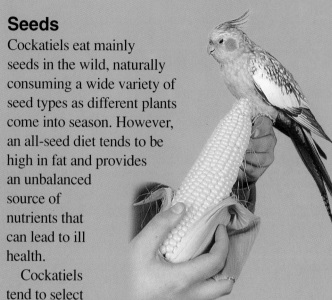

Cockatiels tend to select just one or two seeds from the dozen or more that may be purchased in a mixed bird seed, especially millet and sunflower. These are high in fat and low in calcium and vitamin A. If a smaller amount of a good-quality seed mix is offered, it is likely the bird will eat a greater variety of seed rather than just picking out its favorites and leaving the rest.

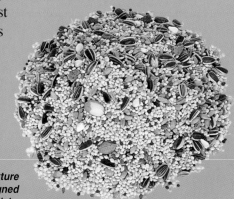

A seed mixture designed for cockatiels.

Quantity

A cockatiel can be maintained on about 1^1/$_2$ to 2 level "measure" tablespoons of seeds per bird, per day, but seeds should be only a part of the overall diet. If there is more than one cockatiel in the cage, separate dishes should be used for each bird to be sure that they all have an opportunity to get to their food. Blow away the husks that are left by the bird as it eats, or it may literally starve in the midst of plenty because it does not realize there is more seed underneath a layer of empty husks.

Food dishes should be cleaned out daily, and the seed stored in a tightly lidded container. Avoid buying very large packs of seed for just one or two birds, as the oil in the seed can easily become rancid.

Regular Supply

Seed hoppers are a good idea. These have a sealed container that is filled with seed, and a small dispenser for the birds to feed from at the bottom. This provides a regular supply of food if the birds have to be left for a while. Similar sealed containers are also available for water, although the water still has to be changed daily.

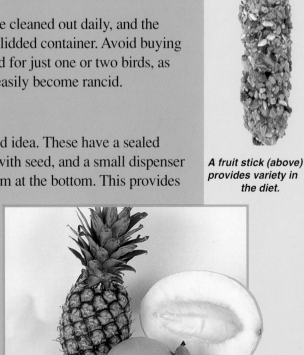

A fruit stick (above) provides variety in the diet.

Fruit and vegetables should make up one quarter of your cockatiel's diet.

13

Feeding Your Cockatiel

Millet is enjoyed, but monitor the amount you give.

A Varied Diet

Cockatiels can actually eat most any of the nutritious foods that humans eat, but only in small quantities. You can offer:

- A little lean meat.

- Cheese.

- Eggs.

- Fruits and vegetables and greens should make up about a quarter of the diet, but they must be washed thoroughly to remove chemicals. They can be fed in manageable chunks, preferably with the skin left on, as it contains many vitamins.

- Pulses, such as chick-peas and beans, soaked overnight and then laid out to sprout, are an excellent food source.

Monitor the amount of food each bird is eating every day, so that you will be quick to notice if one is not eating a balanced diet and can seek veterinary advice if necessary.

Grit

Birds have no teeth and do not chew the seed they eat after dehusking it. It passes down the gullet into a sac called the crop, then it enters the proventriculus, or stomach. It passes on to the gizzard, which is like a muscular grinding machine that contains grit to act as an abrasive. It is therefore essential that caged birds have access to some fine grit that they can eat to aid their digestion.

Grit is an essential aid to digestion.

Minerals

Cockatiels need a high mineral content in their diet, especially in the case of hens that are laying eggs. A cuttlefish bone, attached to the bars of the cage, will exercise the beak as well as supplying a valuable source of calcium.

Egg food is always a favorite.

Cuttlefish bone.

Caring For Your Cockatiel

Cleaning the Cage

Cockatiels need to have their cage cleaned out regularly. The litter or sand on the floor of the cage needs to be changed when it becomes soiled. Sheets of sandpaper are more convenient, but many birds will tear them up, and they seem to enjoy pecking around in bird sand, which also often contains the grit that they need in their crop.

Empty seed husks and uneaten perishable food needs to be removed, and the water changed. If droppings have been deposited around the room after a free flight period, they will not stain furniture if they are removed promptly. Once a week the cage needs a more thorough cleaning, with all furnishings and toys removed and washed, and the bars of the cage wiped with a damp cloth.

Preening

Cockatiels cannot preen themselves properly without being able to wet their feathers, and they naturally enjoy taking a dip. A bowl of water for splashing around is fine, but some cockatiels enjoy being sprayed with an atomizer of lukewarm water.

Cockatiels keep their feathers clean by preening.

Beak and Nails

If the perches are of a suitable diameter and the bird has access to a cuttlefish bone, the beak and nails should wear down naturally and never need clipping.

Nail Care

Overgrown nails may interfere with the bird's ability to perch properly, and will be obvious if they are twisting out at abnormal angles.

   You can clip the nails by holding them up to the light to see the pink quick that runs down the middle of the nail, and leaving about an eighth of an inch (3 mm) above that. If this is your first cockatiel, ask an experienced bird-keeper to help you. Ordinary nail clippers can be used for the task.

Ask an experienced bird-keeper to show you how to clip the nails.

Beak Care

An overgrown beak can be more serious if it interferes with the bird's ability to pick up and dehusk its seed. Sometimes the upper and lower beaks grow completely out of alignment, and may then need clipping very often. It is best to ask a veterinarian to do this, at least for the first time, so that you can see what is involved.

Training

With patient training, the cockatiel will learn to hop onto your hand.

Let your new cockatiel settle in for a day or two before you begin trying to handle it. A cockatiel learns best if it bonds with one particular member of the family, and, providing it is purchased young enough, your cockatiel will learn to regard you as another member of its flock. Lots of regular attention from the beginning will help to make the bird more tame.

Hand-training

The first step in training a cockatiel is to get it used to coming onto a finger. Get the bird used to having your hand in the cage, and then put your outstretched index finger in front of its perch. It may well hop onto your finger, or you can gently push upwards on its body with your finger to encourage it. Cockatiels rarely bite, and although the nip from the beak of a youngster may make your eyes water a bit, it is unlikely to cause any great harm.

You should get to the stage where the bird happily hops onto your finger before letting it out, so that you can return it to its cage with ease. You can also introduce your hand into the cage with a tasty treat, such as a grape, until the bird gets used to the intrusion and accepts the reward. You should then progress to getting the cockatiel used to being held in one hand. First accustom the bird to being stroked on its cheek, next to being stroked along its back, and then to having a hand gently laid upon it. You can then grasp the bird safely in the palm of the hand, with the first and second fingers controlling its head. Your other fingers and thumb should restrain the wings so they do not flap excessively. Any minor procedures such as nail and beak clipping, or the administration of medicines can be carried out in this way.

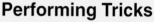
You can teach your bird to say his name.

Performing Tricks

Cockatiels can be taught to perform such tricks as "Ring a bell" and "Climb up a ladder," using actions of the finger that the bird will learn to mimic. Reward positive behavior with a tasty treat. This type of training can be great fun, and helps to build up a bond between the bird and its owner.

It's Good to Talk...

Training a cockatiel to talk requires patience and persistence. Teaching the bird its name is a good place to start – so go for something easy to repeat! The word must be repeated over and over and always with the same pronunciation and emphasis. A lot of cockatiels do not learn to talk. Others will learn to mimic sounds around the house, such as the telephone ringing or even a dog barking.

Breeding

You will need an aviary or a very large cage for a pair of cockatiels to successfully breed and rear their young. Although they are able to reproduce from about six months of age, it is generally accepted that it is best to allow them to pair off and mate once they have reached a year. While some parrots are picky about their choice of partner, cockatiels seem to accept any suitable mate.

Nesting Box

In the wild, cockatiels nest in holes in rotting or dead trees, so you will need to supply a suitable nesting box. This can be purchased from a pet store, or built out of hardwood or exterior grade plywood. It needs to be about 1 foot wide, 10 inches deep and 1 foot tall (30 x 25 x 30 cm). The entrance hole should be about 3 inches (7 cm) in diameter, with a sturdy perch below. The roof or the back should be hinged for cleaning and inspection. Wood shavings in the base of the box will be fine as a nesting material.

Diet

The hen will need a high-quality diet, with extra protein, calcium, and vitamins, in the form of hard-boiled eggs (including some shell), fruit, vegetables, and some meat and dairy produce. She will generally lay four to seven white eggs, one every other day, and will spend a lot of time in the nesting box with them.

Caring for the Clutch

Once the clutch has been laid, the male will do his share of sitting on the eggs, often caring for them during the day while the mother looks after them at night. Provide a bath in the main cage, as they will often return into the nesting box with wet feathers to keep the eggs slightly damp. The eggs should hatch after 17 to 21 days, although, in the first clutch, not all will be fertile.

The Young

The youngsters are tiny and featherless when they are born, but they develop very quickly, reaching nearly half their adult weight within a week, and by six weeks of age are fully fledged and ready to fly.

Cockatiels breed readily in captivity.

Leaving Your Cockatiel

Cockatiels need human company, particularly if they are kept singly. If a bird in this situation is left alone, it will pine. Leaving a radio switched on will help for short periods, however, a cockatiel should not be left unsupervised for more than a day or two. Food needs to be added regularly, empty husks must be cleared away, and the bird must be checked to be sure it is not showing any signs of being ill.

A cage is fairly easy to transport, so you can always take your cockatiel to a friend who could care for it while you are away. Leave clearly written instructions of your bird's requirements and comments from your veterinarian, if relevant.

DID YOU KNOW?

The Lutino form of the cockatiel was first bred in Florida by a Mrs. Moon in the late 1950s, so the birds were originally called "Moonbeams."

Cockatiels on the Move

You may well need to transport your cockatiel from time to time, at least to a veterinary clinic when it is not well.

Some people do take their pet birds on vacation with them, which is fine in a van or similar vehicle, but they must not be left in excessively hot temperatures for any length of time, or they can suffer from heatstroke.

A water spray can help to keep the bird cool during a particularly hot journey.

DID YOU KNOW?

All parrots have zygodactylous feet - which means that unlike most other birds they have two toes pointing forward and two pointing back, whereas others have three pointing forward and two back. This gives them unique gripping power and the ability to pick up food items with their feet and hold them in their beaks.

Cockatiels thrive on human company and will pine if they are left alone.

Health Care

Signs of Illness

● Behavior – a sick cockatiel will be depressed and disinterested in its surroundings, and go off its food.
● Feathers – become ruffled and untidy if the bird is not well.
● Vent – may become sore and caked with droppings.
● Eyes – may become dull or inflamed.
● Breathing – may become noisy and labored, with a discharge from the nostrils.
● Feet – may become swollen, or the cockatiel may perch on only one leg.

Cockatiels can deteriorate very quickly when they are ill, so regular inspection and prompt veterinary treatment are essential if the bird does appear ill. If you have more than one bird, isolate the sick one, and keep it in a cage somewhere really warm until you can get it to a veterinarian. If the bird is not eating, you may be able to encourage it to take a little honey dissolved in water with

DID YOU KNOW?

A survey showed that only one in 52 cockatiels had a vocabulary of over 100 words, and the average talking cockatiel had a vocabulary of 19 words – pretty poor compared to most of the larger parrots.

a dropper, but do not force it to take the fluids against its will or it may inhale the fluid and develop pneumonia.

Administering Medicine

Getting medication into a sick cockatiel is not easy. Some antibiotics come in the form of a soluble powder that can be added to the drinking water, but it can be difficult to make sure enough is taken. Medicated seed is an excellent way of administering drugs if the bird is eating, or drops can be given directly into the mouth. In some cases, the only possible method of administration is by injection.

> ### DID YOU KNOW?
>
> Cockatiels were first introduced in Europe in the 1840s from Australia, and were soon breeding readily.

Bumblefoot

This is the name given to a bacterial infection of the foot, causing it to become inflamed, swollen and tender. This can be very painful for the bird. Perches of the wrong diameter can play a part in causing the problem, and obesity will obviously aggravate it by putting more weight on the feet. In this case, the patient will need to cut down on fattening foods such as millet. A prolonged course of antibiotic treatment is often needed to cure it.

Egg Binding

Female birds will often lay eggs even in the absence of a mate, although they will obviously be infertile. Removing the eggs will simply encourage her to lay more to replace them, so leaving them for her to try and incubate may be best. Sometimes an egg becomes stuck inside the hen, which will cause her to strain to try and pass it. It may be visible just inside the cloaca. Veterinary assistance is usually necessary to try and clear the egg. Sometimes it is even necessary to remove it surgically.

Digestive Disorders

If your bird's droppings are very watery, an abnormal color, or even tinged with blood, this could be due to enteritis, an inflammation of the bowel. A sudden change of diet may bring about the condition, and mild cases may settle down with a change back to just plain seed.

More severe diarrhea may be due to an infection, and sometimes a veterinarian may need to carry out a laboratory examination of the droppings to establish the cause. Antibiotic seed is often given to clear any bacterial infections, and a medicine known as a probiotic can then be added to the drinking water to reestablish the normal, healthy bacteria in the bowel. Parasites such as roundworms and tapeworms may also show up on a fecal examination, and can cause loss of condition and loose droppings. Liquid worming medication is available for birds.

DID YOU KNOW?

Cockatiels generally live to 12 to 14 years of age, but have been known to reach over 20.

Sour Crop

Sour-crop is a term given to an infection of the sac that is used to store the seed after it has been swallowed, and will cause the bird to keep regurgitating foul-smelling food. A dilute solution (2 percent) of an antiseptic in the drinking water may clear the problem, but antibiotics from a veterinarian are often needed.

Feather Loss

This can be due to one of many possible causes, including parasites such as red mites and feather lice, although these are not common in pet cockatiels. French molt is a condition that affects mainly young birds, where the feathers are deformed, often to the point where the bird is unable to fly. It is thought to be caused by a virus. Unfortunately, there is no known cure, although affected birds may be helped with a highly nutritious diet.

Perhaps the most common cause of feather loss in pet cockatiels is feather plucking due to boredom, which can develop to the point where the bird plucks itself bald. Increasing the amount of stimulation and company that the bird receives may help, but in severe cases it may be necessary to fit the bird with a small plastic collar around its neck to restrain it until the habit is broken.

Respiratory Problems

Psittacosis is the most serious disease that affects members of the parrot family. Although it often causes only mild respiratory signs in cockatiels, it can produce a severe form of pneumonia if passed on to humans. Fortunately, it is only common in newly imported birds, so its incidence in pet cockatiels is very rare.

There are several other causes of respiratory infections in pet cockatiels, causing noisy and labored breathing, often with a bubbly discharge from the nostrils. Prompt treatment with antibiotics by a veterinarian is essential as the condition can often be fatal.

Common Ailments

Wounds

Wounds can be caused by fighting between birds, which is quite rare in the peaceable cockatiel, or from injuries sustained within the cage or while flying.

Flesh wounds can be bathed in a mild antiseptic solution daily until they heal. However, they must be kept under close inspection for signs of infection such as an unpleasant smell or discharge that may indicate antibiotic treatment is needed.

Fractures of the wing or foot bones do occur from time to time, and can usually be treated with a splint by a veterinarian.

Surgery for Cockatiels

Birds present particular difficulties to a veterinarian trying to anesthetize them, and there is no doubt that they are at a higher surgical risk than many other animals. Despite this, it is now not uncommon for surgical procedures such as tumor removal to be successfully carried out in cockatiels.

There are veterinarians that have a special interest in the treatment of birds, and if your own veterinarian is reluctant to perform an operation despite there being some realistic hope of success, you could ask to be referred to an avian veterinarian who has the specialized expertise and equipment needed.

But beware – the cost of this type of treatment is likely to be many times the cost of buying a new bird!